106 Ways Parents Can Help Students Achieve

106 Ways Parents Can Help Students Achieve

American Association of School Administrators

Parents as Partners Series

Rowman & Littlefield Education
Lanham, Maryland • Toronto • Plymouth, UK
2006

**Published in partnership with the
American Association of School Administrators
801 N. Quincy Street, Suite 700
Arlington, VA 22203
(703) 528-0700 / www.aasa.org**

Published in the United States of America
by Rowman & Littlefield Education
A Division of Rowman & Littlefield Publishers, Inc.
A wholly owned subsidary of The Rowman & Littlefield Publishing
Group, Inc.
4501 Forbes Boulevard, Suite 200, Lanham, Maryland 20706
www.rowmaneducation.com

Executive Director: Paul D. Houston
Associate Executive Director: Claudia Mansfield Sutton
Editor: Ginger R. O'Neil, GRO Communications
Copy Editor: Liz Griffin
Designer: Jim McGinnis, Mac Designs
Typist: Sabrena Walston

ISBN: 978-0-87652-239-4 / 0-87652-239-8

♾™ The paper used in this publication meets the minimum requirements
of American National Standard for Information Sciences—Permanence
of Paper for Printed Library Materials, ANSI/NISO Z39.48-1992.
Manufactured in the United States of America.

106 Ways Parents Can Help Students Achieve

After more than 30 years of research, the link between parental involvement and higher student achievement is undeniable. For children to succeed, parents must take an active role in their education.

After reviewing more than 80 studies on the impact of parental involvement in education, researchers Anne T. Henderson and Nancy Berla (1995) have found, "The evidence is now beyond dispute. When parents are involved in their children's education at home, their children do better in school."

This publication offers 106 ways parents and others can become more involved in children's education. None of them requires a teaching certificate, and none is costly. What they do involve is a commitment of time and attention . . . and all can pay off in improved educational achievement for your child.

Of course, parents alone can't satisfy their children's every need. And, by themselves, schools can't make sure our students are prepared to be successful in the world of the future. Instead, it will require a partnership — parents, schools, business leaders, and the community working together to prepare our children for the future.

The ideas in this book are grouped in categories, but many could be placed in several sections. We suggest you read through the ideas, and choose one or two to try out. We are sure you'll find your efforts rewarding — for you and your child.

# Learning Begins at Home

Between birth and age 18, children spend just 9 percent of their time in school. That's why your home environment is so important. Here are some ways you can help your children learn at home:

1.

Establish routines for your child. Children thrive on orderliness. Keep a fairly regular schedule for meals, play, and work time. Set a regular bedtime. A child who is used to a routine at home can adapt to classroom rules more easily.

2.

Spend time every day talking with your child about her[1] interests, hobbies, and friends. Children learn language at home and spoken language gives children the foundation for better reading and writing. As children grow older, they need daily conversations as a way to develop values, test ideas, and share their thoughts.

3.

Give your child responsibilities at home. These might include:
* Keeping his bedroom tidy;
* Sharing responsibility for a pet; or
* Doing at least one thing daily for the good of the whole family — washing dishes, picking up the living room, or washing the car.

---

[1] Because we believe in the importance of individuals, we often use the singular pronoun. To be fair, we alternate the use of "him" and "her" throughout this publication.

4

Play games that reinforce language skills. Try question/answer games in which one player tries to learn facts by asking questions.

5

Make sure you have plenty of reading material in your home. Library visits can provide a constant supply of books. Newspapers and magazines can also catch a child's interest. If possible, consider giving your child a subscription to a children's or youth's magazine.

6

Consider holding family meetings. At these meetings, you can discuss plans and dreams. You can also involve children in solving family problems. Older children may want to assume the responsibility of chairing the family meeting.

7

Decorate your child's room with a large map of your state, the United States, or the world. These colorful, inexpensive maps brighten up a room and can help everyone in the family learn more about geography.

8

Set limits on how much television your child can watch and how much time she can spend playing video games. At a minimum, turn off the television during study time. Consider making a rule that there will be no television until all schoolwork is finished. One parent says her family has a rule that no one — parents included — watches TV during study hours. So far, she says, it has been worth the sacrifice. "Children cannot concentrate on two things at one time," she said. "If they only have one thing to think about they certainly get it done a lot faster."

9

Display your child's schoolwork. Many families use the refrigerator for this purpose. Others install a bulletin board on a child's bedroom door. Let your child know you are proud of what he accomplishes in school.

10

Talk about school every day. Ask specific questions — what was the funniest thing that happened today? What was the hardest thing you did today? What new fact/idea did you learn today?

Boost Your Grade on Parent Involvement

A 1997 poll of teachers found that just 18 percent would give a grade of A or B to the parents of students in their schools . . . and 70 percent gave parents a grade of C or D. (The Fourth Phi Delta Kappa Poll of Teachers' Attitudes Toward the Public Schools, *Phi Delta Kappan*, November 1997)

▲

Making Sure Your Child Starts School Ready to Learn

Educators and others have become increasingly aware that a child's experiences during the first five years of life set the stage for later school achievement. School readiness is so important to school success that it is the first of the National Education Goals. Yet, according to the National Education Goals Panel report *Ready Schools* (1998), parents and kindergarten teachers are worried because "a significant number of the children entering elementary school are not ready to learn."

Parents play the most critical role in ensuring that their children come to school ready to learn. Here are a few ways to start your child off on the right track:

11

Even if you think your baby is too young to understand what you are saying, talk anyway. Children develop language abilities earlier when their families talk to them from the first moments of life.

12

Help your child learn letters and numbers. Using crayons, make colorful posters of the "Letter of the Week" or the "Number of the Month." Use clear self-stick paper to turn some of these posters into place mats. Your child can have breakfast with the letter "A," and dinner with the number "7."

13

Help your child learn to recognize shapes. For example, show her that her door is a rectangle, and that an orange is round. Besides teaching shapes, you'll also be making your child a better observer of the world around her.

14

Read aloud to your child regularly and often. *The Read-Aloud Handbook* and *Hey! Listen to This: Stories to Read Aloud,* both by Jim Trelease (available at many libraries or bookstores) provide excellent suggestions. Set a goal of reading to your child for 60 minutes a week — but not necessarily all at one sitting.

15

Count with your child. Kids love to count. Make counting a game. Count the steps between your front door and the bus stop. Count the number of socks in your child's drawer. Count the number of cats you see on your way to the park.

16

Give your child plenty of chances to learn by doing. Let him try new things. Give him simple directions to follow. Whether your child is learning to walk or to tie his shoe, give him lots of time to repeat new activities.

17

Sing songs with your child. Children love the rhythm and rhyme of music. Whether you sing children's songs or your favorite music, you'll be introducing your child to a love of language and music.

18

Teach your child patience. Let him know that sometimes he has to wait for something. It is not always possible — or advisable — for parents to give children what they want. Teach your child that rewards often come only after hard work and effort.

 # Making Family Time Learning Time

In today's hectic world, families often spend more time apart than together. This is why it is important to devote some individual time to each child every day and to spend quality time together as a family. Here are some activities that will bring your family closer together . . . and set the stage for better learning in school:

19

Plan activities the whole family can enjoy: A picnic in the park, a trip to the zoo, a visit to an art gallery, or a hike. These family activities can broaden your children's interests — and add to their intellectual stimulation, imagination, and academic achievement.

> "A parent's job is not so much to teach a child how to read, but to make him want to read."
>
> **Priscilla Vail, learning specialist**

20

To celebrate the new year, a birthday, or another special occasion, consider putting together a "time capsule" — a collection of items that preserve family memories. You'll need to find a sturdy container that will hold your family souvenirs. Invite your children to decorate the container with their artwork, a collage of newspaper articles, or pictures cut from magazines.

Here are some things you might include:

✓ Photos of family members, friends, and pets

✓ Favorite cartoons or comic strips

✓ A favorite T-shirt

✓ Newspaper or magazine clippings about current events

✓ Personal statistics (height, weight, age, school grade level)

✓ Family autographs

✓ School pictures

✓ Copies of report cards

✓ Favorite old toys no longer being used

Once you have assembled your time capsule, "bury" it in the back of the closet. Then enjoy it in future years.

21

Read to or with your children daily. Studies show this is the single most important thing parents can do to help their children achieve. Encourage older children to read to their younger siblings (or to you while you cook dinner). This way, both are developing a habit of reading and listening while forming a special bond with each other.

22

Make reading special. On a winter evening, pop some popcorn and snuggle up together with a book. Or, during the summer, plan a reading picnic under the stars. Give your child a book by a favorite author for a birthday or holiday gift.

23

Have your child use her imagination to plan a trip around the world. Have her think of places she would like to visit. Then help her find out as much as she can about those places. Take a trip to the library where she can find books and articles. On the Internet, she can use a search engine to find out information and perhaps even to read newspapers from places she's studying. Ask the librarian if there are fiction books by authors from these places. Your local video store may also have videos about your child's chosen places.

Teach your child how to write for information about other places. For example, most states have a department of tourism in the state capital she can write to. And most countries have an embassy that can provide your child with additional information.

24

Make sure you and your child have library cards and include a trip to the library in your weekly schedule. Be sure to have a specific place at home for your child to put books when he's not reading them and write the titles and due dates on the family calendar to avoid fines.

25

Kids learn by asking questions, but parents can't possibly have all the answers. And it's good for your child to see that you are still learning too. When your child asks a question you can't answer or would like to explore further, jot it down (or have your child write it) in a small notebook. The next time you're in the library, choose one or two of the questions and try to find the answers. Or, sit with your child when he's online and see what resources are available on the Internet that can help answer these questions.

26

Take a walk through your neighborhood at least once a week. Talk about what you see . . . or about anything that's on your child's mind. These walks will become especially important as she grows older. Establishing the habit of communication when your child is younger can build bridges that will promote talking and listening when she reaches the teenage years.

Studies of individual families show that what the family does is more important to student success than family income or education. This is true whether the family is rich or poor, whether the parents finished high school or not, and whether the child is in preschool or in the upper grades.

– *Strong Families, Strong Schools,* U.S. Department of Education, 1994

27

Learn a new sport or activity with your child. Show your child that learning is a lifelong activity. As your child grows older, let him choose the activity you will learn together.

 Using the Newspaper for Better Learning (or, What's Black and White and Read All Over?)

The daily newspaper provides a source of inexpensive, but valuable, learning activities. And getting children into the habit of reading the newspaper will benefit them throughout life. Here are some ways you can use the newspaper to help your child achieve:

28

Choose a "person of the week." Cut out a photo of this newsmaker and place it in a prominent place. During the week, encourage your child to read as much as she can about the person. Try to include a range of male and female celebrities, athletes, and world leaders of all nationalities and races.

29

Use the weather map to learn geography. Check out the temperature in the cities where relatives and friends live.

30

Help your child use information from the newspaper to make charts and graphs. A young sports fan can track batting averages. A future financial analyst can chart fluctuations in the stock market.

31

Discuss an editorial on a controversial issue with your child. Discuss whether you agree or disagree with the point of view expressed. Then, listen to your child's point of view. Encourage him to write a letter to the editor in response to what you read. This is a good way to share and explore values.

32

Understanding sequence is an important reading skill. Cut comic strips into individual panels. Have young children place them in the correct order. Or, for older children, follow a news story for a week and discuss how and why events unfolded as they did.

33

Look through the newspaper to learn about free activities in your community. You may find out about concerts, plays, storytellers, dance performances, and other opportunities to learn and have fun. Plan to enjoy one of these activities with your family.

Using Computers to Promote Learning

Computers can open up the entire world to your child. And in many families, kids know more about computers than their parents do! But parents must be involved with their children's computer use just as they are involved with other aspects of their child's learning. Here are some tips for making computers an asset to your child's education:

34

Set rules for how much time your child can use the computer. In addition to going online or playing computer games, kids need time to read books . . . to play outside . . . to do their schoolwork . . . and just to think and dream.

35

Place your family's computer in a place where you can supervise what your child is doing. You'll worry less (and have less reason to worry) about what your child is seeing if you check occasionally without hovering.

36

Talk about Internet sites that are off-limits and make sure your child knows she can lose computer privileges if she visits these sites. Many Internet service providers offer parents a way to limit the sites children can visit. Check to see whether yours offers this service if it interests you.

37

Make sure your child knows your rules for safe computer and Internet use. These include rules that your child should never:

✓ give out personal information (including name, address, or phone number).

✓ share his password, even with friends.

✓ arrange a face-to-face meeting with someone he meets online unless you approve of the meeting and go with him to a public place.

✓ use bad language or send mean messages online.

✓ answer messages that make him feel confused or uncomfortable, and should tell you or another adult right away if he gets such a message.

38

If you do not have a computer in your home, your child may be able to use free facilities in your community. Check out computer availability at a library or community center, your child's school, or even a local shopping mall, which may have a room with computers for those visiting the mall. Some public housing complexes also have free computer centers with online access for their residents.

> *"What children bring to school . . . is critically important in the learning process."*
>
> – **Dorothy Rich, founder, Home and School Institute**

Increasing Your Child's Self-Esteem and Motivation

Kids who have high self-esteem are willing to take chances in school. They're able to stay with a difficult subject until they master it. And students and adults who make persistent effort are most likely to succeed. Here are some ways you can boost your child's self-esteem:

39

Know your child's strengths and weaknesses. All children are unique. Even in the same family, one child may love math and find it easy, while another finds it a challenge. Some may have trouble concentrating on reading while another constantly has his nose in a book. Challenge kids in their areas of strength and provide support in areas of weakness. One way to better understand your child's strengths and weaknesses is to talk regularly with his teacher or teachers.

40

Praise your child's efforts as well as her accomplishments. When she sets the table, say, "I appreciate the fact that you did that without being asked. You're a hard worker." If your child is doing her homework, say, "You are working hard. I know your work will pay off."

41

Help your child be proud of your family's ethnic heritage. Learn as much as you can about your ancestors' culture. Read books to learn more about your family's roots. Find out about famous people who share your ethnic background. Encourage your child to talk with older relatives to gather family memories.

42

Teach your child to celebrate diversity. Learn more about other cultures. Watch television programs or read books about other countries. Share foods from your family's ethnic tradition and then learn more about foods from other cultures.

43

Find time for one-on-one conversations with your child. Each week, try to set aside some special time. Write it on your calendar so your son or daughter can look forward to it. During this time, do something your child likes — play a game, watch a movie, or go for a walk.

44

Teach your child how to set goals. First, help your child choose one goal that is both challenging and attainable. Examples might be, "I will complete my history reading every night," or "I will receive a grade of 90 on my spelling test." Write the goal on a piece of paper or poster board and post it where your child can see it. A visual reminder will help keep your child motivated.

Next, talk with your child about strategies for accomplishing the goal. These should be concrete steps that help your child move purposefully toward the goal. For example, a child trying to improve a spelling grade might:

✓ set aside 15 minutes of study time every day,

✓ make flash cards of difficult words, and

✓ ask family members to provide practice quizzes.

Talk with your child about her progress. If she completes each step, be sure to celebrate her effort. If she encounters problems, help her get back on track.

Finally, evaluate your child's progress. Did she reach her goal? Why or why not? What did she learn from her success? If she didn't reach her goal, what did she learn from the experience? Praise your child's effort in trying to reach the goal, and let her know that even if she didn't succeed as she'd hoped, she still made positive progress and learned important skills.

Then help her set another achievable goal. Every time your child reaches a goal, she's building her self-esteem so she can try to reach another.

45

Pick your child up when he's down. Remind him that striking out in the baseball game doesn't mean he's a failure at home. Let him know that a poor grade on a spelling test doesn't mean he isn't smart.

46

Be aware of your expectations. Parents who assume boys are "naturally" better at math or sports — and girls better at reading — may be limiting their child's future accomplishments.

47

Encourage your child to take part in extracurricular activities. After-school drama, athletics, music, language, service, and other clubs give kids a chance to try new skills and receive recognition for a job well done.

Supporting Your Child's Schoolwork

By showing interest in your children's learning, and by holding high expectations for your children, you can help them develop attitudes that lead to school success. Here are some ways you can improve your children's academic achievement:

48

Make homework a priority. Provide a quiet, well-lit place for your child to study. Make sure he has the basic "tools of the trade" — a dictionary, a ruler, pens and pencils.

49

Establish a regular study time. Expect your child to spend some time on schoolwork every day. On days when there are no assignments, your child can read a book for the allotted time. During study time, the television should be off. Turn on your telephone answering machine, if you have one — otherwise, take messages so your child can return calls later.

50

If your child has difficulty with one subject, have her begin a homework session by completing that assignment first while she's fresh. She can save her favorite subjects for last.

51

Do your own "homework" while your child is studying, if possible. Pay bills, write letters, or balance your checkbook. When your child see that study time applies to everyone, they'll be more likely to take it seriously.

52

When your child begins to study history, help her create a timeline that will be displayed in her room. One year, have her fill in important dates in American history. The next year, she can add important dates in world history.

53

Today's news is history in the making. Watch the evening news with your child. Talk about current events at the dinner table. Choose one or two stories to follow closely. Read more about them in newspapers and magazines.

54

Consider using the "rule of thumb" when choosing books for your child. Have your child read a page of a book aloud. Each time he encounters a word he doesn't know, have him hold up one finger. If he holds up four fingers and a thumb, finding five or more troublesome words on a page, the book is probably too difficult.

55

Reward your child for doing well. However, keep in mind that always offering money or presents for special accomplishments will leave the impression that people should work only for rewards . . . and not for the pride of doing a job well. Try rewarding outstanding performance with time together. Let your "star" choose an activity for the whole family to enjoy — a picnic, watching a favorite video, or a visit to the zoo.

56

Start a parent-child book club. A small group of parents and children can choose books to read and discuss together. A great resource for starting such a club is Shireen Dodson's (1997) *The Mother-Daughter Book Club*.

57

Help your child do better on tests. Encourage your child to:

✓ Study for several days before a test. Children need time to absorb information, and cramming *doesn't* work.

✓ Get plenty of sleep . . . and a good breakfast.

✓ Listen carefully to directions. (Teachers may deduct points if students don't follow instructions completely.)

✓ Look over the test before answering any questions. Nothing is worse than discovering a 15-minute essay question when you have only 5 minutes remaining in the class.

✓ Pace himself by not spending too much time on any one question. It's usually better to answer as many questions as possible. If there's time, your child can return to questions that have him stumped.

58

Turn your child into the teacher by playing the student. Have your child teach you about her lesson. Doing so will help her absorb important information.

Working With the School

When home and school work together, students learn more. There are many ways parents — even the busiest parents — can establish a partnership with their child's school. Here are some suggestions:

"Children aren't fooled. They know we give time to the things we love."

–John Bradshaw

59

Get to know your child's teachers. This is just as important for high school students as for 1st graders. Take younger children to school on the first day. Each year, send a brief note to the teachers letting them know you want to work together to improve your child's education.

60

Attend parent-teacher conferences. These meetings, usually held twice a year, give parents and teachers a great opportunity to share ideas and solve problems. Here are some questions you might want to ask:

✓ Does my child attend class regularly? Complete assignments regularly?

✓ Does my child follow directions?

✓ What aspects of school does my child seem to enjoy most?

✓ What are my child's strengths and weaknesses?

✓ Does my child need help in any academic area or need to be referred to a school specialist for any reason?

✓ Does my child get along well with other children?

✓ What can I do to help my child?

61

Join your school's parent-teacher association. And try to say "yes" when you're called to help. (Or ask if there's another job you can do.) Your involvement with your child's school will send a message that you think school is important. If every parent spends a little time working with the school, the results can be dramatic.

Joining the parent-teacher association is especially important as children grow older. By working with other parents, you can agree to work together to set rules regarding important issues, such as the need for parental supervision at parties.

62

Compile a list of parents with special skills or interests for your school. These talents can help teachers enrich learning activities for all students. Volunteer to discuss your own career with a group of students.

63

Appear as a "guest reader" and read one of your own favorite books from childhood to your child's class.

64

Stay informed. Attend school events and programs. Read the school newsletter. Attend a school board meeting.

65

Consider spending a day at school with your child. Many working parents schedule a day of annual leave for this purpose. Or join your child for lunch in the school cafeteria.

66

Volunteer. Many studies show that when parents take an active role as school volunteers, student achievement rises. That's particularly true for the children of school volunteers. Your actions really do speak louder than your words.

In an elementary school, you might:

✓ Help tutor a child.

✓ Make a bulletin board.

✓ Read to a child.

✓ Chaperone a field trip.

✓ Listen to a child read to you.

In an intermediate or high school, you might:

✓ Create a welcoming committee for newcomers to the community.

✓ Chaperone a dance or help with security at a game.

✓ Sponsor a chapter of Students Against Drunk Driving or another service organization.

✓ Work in the attendance office telephoning parents about students' absences.

✓ Assist the school nurse.

67

Say "thank you." Jot a quick note to thank a teacher for spending extra time with your son or daughter. Call the principal to share the good news about a history teacher who has sparked your daughter's interest. At the end of the year, write a letter to a teacher who has done an outstanding job — and send a copy to the school district's personnel office.

68

Consider serving on a school or district advisory group. As a parent, you have valuable insights that can help improve education for all children.

69

Don't be afraid to advocate for your child. Perhaps you are concerned about a teacher who assigns too much homework — or not enough. Perhaps your child is persistently unhappy with a teacher. Perhaps you believe your child should be taking more challenging courses. If your concern extends over time, let the school know. Begin by talking with the teacher. If you can't resolve things at that level, contact the principal. Other school administrators, including the superintendent, may also be helpful.

When you act as an advocate for your child, remember that reason and facts are more persuasive than anger and emotion.

Promoting Your Family's Values

Parents today are worried about the values their children are exposed to in society. The schools share this concern. But schools recognize that children's primary values must continue to come from home. Here are some ways to pass on your family's values to your children:

70

Talk about your values. If you choose to visit a relative or spend time with your child rather than work overtime, talk to your child about the fact that you believe building relationships with people is more important than accumulating a lot of things. If you give money to support a cause you believe in, tell your child why you're doing it.

71

Encourage your child to talk about his values, too. Whenever possible, try to support your child's values by taking positive action. For instance, many children are as concerned, if not more concerned, about protecting the environment as adults. If this is the case, you could work with your son or daughter to promote recycling in your family.

72

Think about the message you send with your actions. It's hard to talk about honesty if you brag about cheating on your taxes. It's hard to teach the value of human kindness and fairness if you condemn other races or peoples.

73

Teach your child how to make decisions. Ask your child to think about what might happen if she chooses one course of action over another. But let her make some of her own decisions — and discover her own consequences.

74

Let your child know you are always there to listen. Teens sometimes say they don't talk with their parents because they don't want a lecture. If your son or daughter starts discussing a problem, make an effort to listen more than you talk.

 # Helping Your Child Avoid Negative Peer Pressure

As children grow older, they spend more time with friends. This is a necessary part of growing up as teens learn how to get along outside their families. But peer pressure can lead to unhealthy behavior, including early sexual activity, and drug and alcohol use. In addition to passing on your family's values, here are some ways you can limit the negative influence of peer pressure on your children:

75

Get to know your child's friends. Invite them to spend their after-school hours in your home. For the price of a few refreshments, you'll soon learn about who your child is seeing . . . and you'll be able to make sure no drugs or alcohol are used.

76

Teach your child how to say no. You might roleplay a situation in which your teenager is offered drugs or alcohol. Here are some responses you can model and discuss with your child:

"No, thank you."

"I don't need that to have a good time."

"I have to stay sharp for my team."

" 'No' means 'no.' "

77

Talk with other parents. You will no doubt learn that "everybody" isn't allowing kids to have unsupervised parties. Many schools sponsor parent networks that help parents set limits that apply to everyone. For example, parents in these networks may agree:

✓ not to allow parties in their homes when they are not present.

✓ not to permit the use of drugs in their homes or on their property.

✓ to follow certain guidelines if a party is held at their home, including calling the parents of any child who possesses drugs or alcohol.

✓ to call the parents hosting a party to verify the occasion and location.

78

Turn peer pressure into positive pressure. Encourage your child to work with other teens to tackle a problem in your community. He might volunteer at a soup kitchen, develop a performance for senior citizens, or clean up a stretch of highway. He'll be improving the community and boosting his self-esteem. (He'll also have something to write about in his college-entrance essays.)

79

Many schools sponsor peer counseling programs. Students who are accepted into these programs learn listening and leadership skills, and they often have a chance to work with younger students as positive role models. Find out whether your school has such a program and encourage your child to participate.

Promoting Good Health = Promoting Good Learning

The Greeks knew the importance of a sound mind and body. Today, teachers know that poor health and nutrition can cause poor performance in school. Here are some ways you can help your child stay physically and mentally fit:

80

Exercise together. Studies show that kids in the United States today are more overweight than in any earlier generation. In fact, doctors are now seeing children with adult health problems, like high cholesterol. One of the main reasons children are so overweight, doctors say, is because they don't get enough exercise. Set aside a regular time for your family to enjoy some outdoor activity together. A brisk walk will improve your fitness . . . and give you time to talk with your kids.

81

Encourage your child to take part in an after-school sport. Not only will your child get more exercise, but sports also teach teamwork and build friendships. Be sure to encourage your child to choose a sport (instead of you choosing one for your child). Kids often translate success in sports to success in school.

82

Learn some of the warning signs that your son or daughter may be involved with drugs. These include:

✓ Declining school attendance or performance

✓ Worsened relationships with family and friends

✓ Ignored curfews

✓ Increased borrowing of money from family or friends

✓ Possession of alcohol or drug paraphernalia

✓ Stealing

✓ Hanging around a new group of friends, especially those you suspect use drugs

83

Inhalant use is a particular danger for children in middle school. Kids can use common household products — paint, hair spray, air fresheners, and so on — to achieve a "high." But inhalants can kill suddenly . . . or cause permanent brain damage. The American Academy of Pediatrics notes these common signs of inhalant abuse:

✓ Breath and clothes that smell like chemicals

✓ Nausea and lack of appetite

✓ Paint or stains on body or clothing

✓ Nausea and lack of appetite

✓ Spots and sores in the mouth area

For more information, see www.aap.org/family/inabuse.htm.

84

Help your school develop policies about alcohol and other drug use and abuse. Be sure to include rules that discourage tobacco use. Allow middle and high school students to be a part of establishing these rules.

Preparing Your Child for the World of Work

All parents want their kids to find work that will give them a satisfying and secure life. Here are some important things you can do during the school-age years to help you children prepare for success in the work world:

85

Ask your child to describe her life as an adult. Then have her research what she needs to do now to prepare for a career. A student who wants to become a doctor, for example, needs to take challenging math and science courses in high school.

86

Help your teen make a budget for the kind of adult life he imagines living. How much should he budget for rent (and don't forget the cost of utilities)? How much would it cost to buy a car (don't forget insurance and gas)? Now get out the want ads to look at what different jobs pay. Your teen may find there's a huge gap between the salary he's likely to earn and the life he'd like to live. Explain how the school courses he takes and the grades he earns *now* can affect his earning power.

87

Help your teenager understand that even if she doesn't have a specific career goal, the decisions she makes now can affect her future. Encourage her to take challenging courses, including the optional higher-level math courses. Such courses can make the difference in whether or not your child will be able to attend college or vocational training courses after high school.

88

Make sure your teen keeps reading — language arts ability is one of the greatest predictors of college success.

89

After-school jobs can teach teenagers responsibility. In some families, these jobs are a necessary part of family security. But you must make sure your child isn't placing too much emphasis on work and not enough on school. In the long-run, a solid education is the best investment your child can make in her future.

90

If your child has a job, suggest that some of the money he earns be saved for college or other training, a large purchase such as a car, or a trip to see a friend. Teach him how to handle a checking or savings account.

91

Not every young person needs to go to college. But to be successful, every American worker needs some advanced training. If your
child is not interested in attending college, find out about vocational
schools or other training courses that offer preparation for a rewarding career. Many high schools offer "Tech Prep" programs, which
allow students to begin preparing for a career while still in high
school. Typically, students in these programs spend a year or two in a
community college or vocational school after they graduate before
entering the work world.

 ## Getting the Help You Need

Parenting is a tough job. Odds are, you'll need
some help at some time while your child is
growing up. It's critical that you not be afraid
to ask for help, and that you know who to ask. Here are some places
where you can get help:

92

Talk with your child's school counselor. He or she can often provide
important insight into how well your child is doing in school. A
counselor can also help you work with teachers to address school
problems.

93

Turn to your minister, rabbi, or other religious adviser as a source of
support and help. Many religious organizations sponsor free or low-
cost counseling.

94

Look into community offerings. In a growing number of neighbor-hoods, civic organizations have joined together to provide wholesome after-school activities for children. These range from athletic leagues to computer clubs to homework help. See whether your community offers this kind of after-school program. If not, you might want to work with other parents to see if you can start such a program.

95

Visit your school or public libraries for books on parenting. If you need information on how to deal with a particular age, or on solving a particular problem, you may find the information you need in a book at the library or online.

96

Find out whether your school has a parent center. If so, check there for the latest resources on parenting and how to help your child in school. Many parent centers also offer other services to parents, from high school completion courses to free computer use.

97

Consider joining a parent group. Many community mental health agencies sponsor groups where parents meet to share their concerns and support each other. These groups can be a valuable way to learn new parenting strategies. Seek family counseling when problems seem severe, and be open to suggestions about yourself. All problems are not your child's fault.

*The most accurate predictor of a student's achievement
in school is not income or social status, but the extent to
which that student's family is able to (1) create a home
environment that encourages learning; (2) communicate
high, yet reasonable, expectations for their children's
achievement and future careers; and (3) become
involved in their children's education at school and in
the community.*

— National PTA, National Standards for Parent/Family Involvement
   Programs

Establishing Home/School/Community Support for Learning

Every citizen has a stake in preparing our nation's next generation.
Here are some ways communities can play a more active role in helping students achieve:

98

Establish a community task force to ensure that all children have
access to high-quality, developmentally-appropriate educational
experiences during their preschool years. These might include
home-visit programs to train parents, employer-supported daycare,
or high-quality preschool programs.

99

Establish a school-business partnership. Both partners can work together to share ideas, work toward common goals, and support efforts to help students learn. Employers might consider granting parents leave to attend conferences or volunteer in school, for example. Schools, in turn, can work with the business community to prepare graduates with the skills they will need to enter the workforce.

100

Launch a community effort to ensure that all children have adequate healthcare. Find out what health care services are available. Children whose teeth hurt, or who need glasses, cannot concentrate in school. Ask for local support to fill in the gaps, where they exist.

101

Develop a list of community resources available to help families. Disadvantaged students may need services from many community agencies. A resource directory can make families aware of where to get the help they need. Distribute the list widely to school and agency staff members.

102

Consider cooperative activities to better meet the needs of children and their families. When several agencies cooperate, they can reduce wasteful duplication . . . and improve services. For example, the county health department could schedule regular visits to the school health clinic. Social service workers could meet with school counselors.

103

Remember that retired citizens have much to contribute to the schools. They can visit classrooms to provide an extra pair of eyes and hands for a busy teacher. They can take the time to listen to a troubled student. Those confined to their homes may be able to help teachers prepare special learning activities or materials for bulletin boards.

104

If you need help to improve your own skills, reach out to the business community, which has an interest in ensuring that all workers can read. Worksite literacy programs are an effective way to meet parents' reading needs.

105

Check out public libraries, which are strong educational partners. They can sponsor story hours for preschoolers and their parents, special programs that motivate children to read, or specialized evening classes on topics of interest to parents.

106

Ask churches and civic organizations to provide valuable services for schools. Many are excellent sources of volunteers, and many sponsor evening or after-school tutoring programs for students who need extra help, organize drives to collect school supplies for needy students, and raise funds for scholarships.

Final Thoughts

Clearly, Americans want *all* our children to have the skills they need to be successful in the 21st century. In fact, the 1998 Phi Delta Kappa/Gallup Poll of the Public's Attitudes Toward the Public Schools found that the public would rather spend money on improving public schools (50 percent) than on cutting their own taxes (31 percent).

With a little caring and creativity, parents can help children get ready for, enjoy, and stay in school, and to prepare for a bright future after graduation. It is important to keep in mind, however, that while parents are the most important influence on a child's life, students learn better when schools, families, and communities work together. Only with a concerted effort will students become lifelong learners, and ultimately, happier, more responsible citizens.

Resources

Excellent new resources for parents are published every day. Here are some publications, organizations, and online resources available to help parents help their children.

American Academy of Pediatrics has several health-related publications for parents, which can be found on the Internet at www.aap.org.

Amundson, K.J. (1999). *Getting Your Child Ready for School.* Arlington, Va.: American Association of School Administrators.

Amundson, K.J. (1999). *Helping Your Child Succeed in Elementary School.* Arlington, Va.: American Association of School Administrators.

Amundson, K.J. (1999). *Helping Your Child Succeed in Middle and High School.* Arlington, Va.: American Association of School Administrators.

Amundson, K.J. (1999). *Helping Your Child With Homework.* Arlington, Va.: American Association of School Administrators.

Amundson, K.J. (1999). *Parents, Partners in Education.* Arlington, Va.: American Association of School Administrators.

Amundson, K.J. (1999). *Reading, Writing, Speaking, and Listening Skills: Keys to Your Child's School Success.* Arlington, Va.: American Association of School Administrators.

Communities in Schools, America's largest stay-in-school network, offers resources and ideas for helping America's communities help students at www.cisnet.org.

Dodson, S. (1997). *The Mother-Daughter Book Club.* New York: HarperCollins.

The Family Education Network offers many ideas for parent/school partnering at www.familyeducation.com.

Henderson, A.T. and N. Berla. (1995). *A New Generation of Evidence: The Family Is Critical to Student Achievement.* Washington, D.C.: Center for Law and Education.

KidsCampaigns is an information and action center for adults who want to make their communities work for children. It can be accessed online at www.connectforkids.org.

Leonhardt, M. (1997). *99 Ways to Get Kids to Love Reading*. New York: Three Rivers Press.

Lewis, B.A. (1998). *What Do You Stand For?: A Kid's Guide to Building Character*. Minneapolis: Free Spirit Publishing.

National PTA, National Standards for Parent/Family Involvement Programs. The National PTA also has a number of publications designed to help parents play a more active role in their children's education. These are available online at the PTA's Education Resource Libraries, at www.pta.org.

Rich, D. (1998). *MegaSkills: How Families Can Help Children Succeed in School and Beyond*. Boston: Houghton Mifflin.

Rich, D. (1997). *What Do We Say? What Do We Do?: Helping Our Children Succeed in School and Beyond*. New York: Forge.

Steinberg, L. and A. Levine. (1997). *You and Your Adolescent: A Parent's Guide for Ages 10 to 20*. New York: HarperPerennial.

Trelease, J. (1992). *Hey! Listen to This! Stories to Read Aloud*. New York: Penguin Books.

Trelease, J. (1982). *The Read-Aloud Handbook*. New York: Penguin Books.

U. S. Department of Education has many free publications for parents on a wide range of subjects. They are available by calling 1-800-USA-LEARN or on the Internet at www.ed.gov/pubs/parents.

Acknowledgments

106 Ways Parents Can Help Students Achieve is a copublication of the American Association of School Administrators (AASA), 801 N. Quincy Street, Suite 700, Arlington, VA 22203. The association, founded in 1865, is the professional organization for school superintendents, central-office administrators, principals, university administrators and professors, and others across the United States, Canada, and other parts of the world.

Author Kristen J. Amundson, a leading education writer in the Washington, D.C., metropolitan area, has written extensively on parent–children concerns.

AASA is grateful to Anne T. Henderson, who continues to document the clear and convincing link between parent involvement and student achievement, and to Dorothy Rich, founder of the Home and School Institute, for her groundbreaking work on why and how schools and families can work together to improve education for all children.